In Too Deep

First American
Book In Print

Poetry and Prose

Written by

Ralph Watkins

Publisher: AUDAX, LLC.
All Copyrights Reserved copyright 2014
Email: dmvpoet@gmail.com
Published District Heights, M.D.
Print In September 2019

PREFACE

FIRST EDITION OF BOOK OF POETRY *IN TOO DEEP* WRITTEN BY RALPH WATKINS JR. DESIGNED FOR FAMILY, FRIENDS AND PEOPLE OF MATURE AGE; THAT LOVE READING MODERN, AND URBAN LITERARY CREATIVE WORK. WHICH EMBODIES THOUGHTS, FEELINGS AND EMOTIONS. OFTEN REFLECTING ON LIFE, FAMILY, AND RELATIONSHIPS EXPERIENCES.

THE BODY OF WORK STRETCHES OVER 40 YEARS, FROM EARLY CHILDHOOD TO PRESENT, WHICH ENCOMPASSES AND DEPICTS VARIOUS LIFE SITUATIONS. POETRY HAS ALWAYS BEEN A USEFUL TOOL TO SHARE, AND ENCOURAGE OTHERS. AND IT ALSO BUILD BRIDGES BETWEEN TWO DIFFERENT PLACES, TO GIVE PEOPLE AN EASIER AND SAFER PASSAGE THROUGH WORDS ON A PAGE.

ONE OF MY BIGGEST DREAMS, GOES AS FAR BACK AS I CAN REMEMBER, AND THAT IS TO BE A CREATIVE WRITER OF POETRY AND SHORT STORIES. I DID NOT TAKE A DIRECT PATH, AND I WAS NOT ALWAYS FOCUSED. BUT MY HEART WAS ALWAYS IN THE RIGHT PLACE. IN MY HEART, I KEPT THIS LOVE FOR WRITING POETRY ALIVE. OVER THE YEARS I WOULD REVISIT THE THOUGHT OF WRITING A COMPLETE BOOK OF POETRY.

I HAVE ARRIVED AT A PLACE IN MY HEART, WHEREAS I NO LONGER WANT TO PUT OFF MY DREAM UNTIL TOMORROW. GOOD LUCK MY FRIENDS IN YOUR TRAVELS THROUGH THIS WORLD.

TABLE OF CONTENTS

You Stopped Loving Me

You stopped loving me and I don't know why. You stopped caring about me, and I don't know why.

Nothing I say or do seem to matter much to you. When I stop to listen for all the things you do not say, I don't hear you say, I love you or how beautiful I am. So, I looked into the mirror and took a long hard look at myself.

Many of my youthful appearances have gone, but I am still the same person inside. Then I realized some people are only attracted to by what they see, I didn't know that I was undressing in front of a blind person. Anyone that can not see you inside out, needs to be shown the front door, and kicked out.

Keep Your Pet

Most people aren't up front. I don't like dogs. I don't like cats. I don't like any domesticated animals. They are not cute, And should never be hugged or kissed. There, I said it.

Most animal Lovers say, "I'm keeping my pet and you can leave." they don't know That just saved us a lot of time, money and unnecessary future arguments.

We all have to recognize and respect each others differences, even if that means having to move on.

A Bad Dream

This morning I woke up and I screamed, and I called for my mommy and daddy, because I was having a bad dream.

I rose up, waiting for either one, but neither one came into my room to hold me, and let me know, everything is going to alright.

It took me a minute to realize, I'm a grown man now, and my mommy lives in another town. And my daddy is dead asleep.

I sat there afterwards, and thought how wonderful it was, when they use to come into my bedroom, and would chase all the monsters away.

A Chance

If you have a chance to be happy, and put on a smile, try your best to wear it well. We all know how heavy the heart can get, when someone you know and love passes away; its weight is more than a truck load. Life is way too short to walk around angry all the time. After awhile you forget why you were even mad.

I remember in the beginning the promise we made, that we'd never go to bed mad at each. Somehow that never comes back to mind, until they can't see you looking up; but every tear imaginable is falling, while you are looking down.

I know what you were both thinking, "One day we'll makeup, and things will go back to the way they were."

To so many, looking down or laying down facing up, that tomorrow never came. As my father would say, "Find a way to makeup with your brother or sister."

I'd always walk away with my head hung down, thinking as a child, this is way too hard. But, when I found myself looking down, it was way too late to make amends. I knew then, I had truly let my father down.

A Race Against Me

A race against the old me, there's no doubt who would win.

Today's Ralph would win. Yesterday's Ralph was incredibly fast, but he wasn't ambitious.

Today's Ralph runs with more heart, and determination. Yesterday's Ralph ran 10-15 miles and got nothing out of it.

Today's Ralph takes a page from every previous experience to push even further.

One good thing could be said about the young Ralph, if it wasn't for him, I wouldn't be here today.

No Music

For the first time in a long time, I ran without music. I couldn't find my iPod, but I didn't stress over running without it either.

I heard everything; cars whistling pass me, emergency sirens from a distance and the closing of front porch doors from people leaving out of their homes in the morning.

All of this, was almost scary, because I've normally shut this world out when I am running.

Without my playlist, I didn't pick up my pace along the way, at certain intervals.

Its all good, I made it back home without falling or any loose dog giving chase, "Ain't nobody got time for that!"

New Day

A new day
I am trying to
break in new strides,
disregarding the temperature.
I have to go by how I feel.

That's why I like to get dressed
before I look out the window.
My determining factors are,
am I breathing, my heart beating
and can I still see the vision
that God has put in me?

It's time, before it's too late.
We know this time, we can never
get back.

It's Cold Outside

Its cold outside

but I'm not bitter.

No matter how bad life gets,

I'm no quitter.

Even when I'm in

a disagreement with

a woman, I'm no hitter.

I've had my moments

on the field in the game,

it doesn't bother me to

be a sitter.

When I'm driving along, and

I see a space where I can get in,

I'm a fitter.

But the one thing I can't stand

is when other people stop along the

highway to litter.

Nothing

Nothing stands taller, bigger or
more undetermined in front
of you, than you.
You are your biggest obstacle
in life.
Wake up!
I still have a lot to learn
about myself.
If I knew more about
myself, it's no telling
what I am capable of.
There has been certain
times in my life I didn't
take the next step or
the leap of faith.
I stopped and watched
many others like me
go forward.
I ask myself many times
over, what is that
thing inside of me
that switches into
an off position?
If it's fear, what am I
afraid of?

I know that you'll never
become successful at
anything in life, if you
don't learn about
yourself first.
The best way to learn
about yourself is not
to be a quitter in life,
face the task ahead,
find a way to triumph
over the hurdles in
everyday life. Believe
that it's within you
to win or to become
successful.

R A W

Luke's Law

My dad didn't play any games when it came to other people, with us as his children. He didn't allow anyone to hit, spank, raise their voices or mistreat us in any kind of way. He made it perfectly clear to everyone and to us and he took that very seriously and to his grave. But, I didn't let that spirit amongst other things, die with him.

I felt entrusted to keep certain things alive. Don't mess with my children. I've taught them to be very respectful, don't take anything that does not belong to them and be where you suppose to be, And most importantly, scream for help and I'll always come to your rescue but don't be in the wrong when I get there.

But still, you're my child and no one earthly born should or will put their hands on you, other than me. My father meant that from his heart, with all good intentions, or that person would have him and hell to pay.

When it comes to seeing someone angry, I've only seen lightning up close and coming from my dad's eyes. He didn't play, and it mattered; these are my children, and no one has a right to put their hands on any of them. I could tell you a few stories but I am trying to let my dad rest in peace. And let those bodies remain where they are buried.

Why Are You Worrying

Why are you worrying?
Why are you crying?
When you're covered by the blood,
and you have greatness
at your side.
He is your forward God
He is your rear God
He is your everything God
If you put it in His hands,
and leave it there.
He is the Alfa and the Omega.
He is the God of peace.
Just take one step at a time
in the newness and fullness
and you'll be amazed.
Put on the whole armor of God,
then you'll be able to taste
and see the goodness of His love.

When You Love

When you love something
you don't ever stop.
You have to keep the romance
going for as long you can.
It's okay to run a little faster,
work a little harder, and take
those strides forwards
while gasping out for air.

At the end of the day, I could not say
to myself I didn't try when I had the
chance within my reach and I let the other
runners pass me by.

How can you say you love something,
and deny yourself the victory?
Winning take everything you have inside of you
and more. A lot of days we're looking for good weather
and other outside chances to win.

We have to build our strength, developed a plan for success, stay focused at all times but more importantly, we have to have a purpose and a winning attitude. The road ahead is long and the work is hard, And a lot of times you're going to feel like giving up.

It's then you have to reach within yourself and find those things that allows us to push even further ahead. This is an endless process. But when you truly love something. You can never just sit back and imagine what victory would tastes like.

Coloring

Coloring with my crayons
Trying to stay inside the lines.
I only get three crayons at
a times. I picked blue, green
and yellow.
They told me I can have any three
crayon in the box, but
I can't have red.
Of course, after getting up out
of my seat and walking across
the room, not being able to
to get my choice color.
Somewhere along the way, I
through a complete tantrum.
Before I settled down, things in
that room were everywhere.
I looked down at my feet and
saw the red Crayola crayon they
wouldn't give to me.
I picked it up, smiled and walked
back to my seat. In a few minutes, I am going
to want a juice box before my nap time.

This Whole World Is Crazy

This whole world is crazy
I wish I could set it
on fire.
Every time I fall out
of love, and there is
no one I desire.
I want to be in love
but it doesn't seem
to work for me.
When I'm alone,
I'm constantly looking
for someone to fill
the void space in
my life.
That doesn't always work,
it's always end up looking
like an ugly piece of Art
Work that no one wants.
I know beautiful, I watched
beautiful come off my
canvas, and walk away.

The Dream

Dr. Martin Luther King had a dream
that included himself,
the people around him,
for that day,
for our tomorrow.
The dream was so strong
it empowered others to believe
in his dream and follow him.
It wasn't about being Black
or anyone hating Whites.
It was dream of equality.
The dream is still alive, and
we're still struggling for equality.
It can't be only one man's dream.
We all have to march together with
Dr. Martin Luther King, until this dream
is alive with everyone, everywhere,
regardless of race, gender, age or
sexual orientations.

Had Our Differences

My dad and I had our differences.
He said, Son, we are going to have differences.
but, unfortunately I am going to always be
right.

You might not like what I am telling you, and I
don't really care. The only thing that is im-
portant to me is that you recognize the differ-
ences and do as I ask.

When you feel that you no longer want to lis-
ten, or follow directions, pack all your stuff and
just leave.

Your mom and I have provided you with a roof
over your head, food on the table and decent
clothes on your back. I don't think we should
have any differences son.

Turned Off the Lights

I figure, if I stay home, lock the doors and turn off all the lights, I wouldn't get into any trouble. I will just sit here and write, and listen to the sounds outside.

Not even two hours into my therapeutic day off; I hear yelling outside my window, knocking on my door, "I know you're in there mofo'." I knew I forgot one other thing, I should parked my vehicle several blocks away.

I only went outside to let them know that this is a quiet zone community." Nonetheless I started celebrating because wanted me to help him finish a dime bag of weed whereas it's now legal in Colorado.

Police pulls up minutes later, to inform us that they had received a disturbance call from this resident. And, reminded us after several citations, that this is not Colorado. And, when they do legalize it, he'll join us.

Uncontrollable

I am uncontrollable but I'd like to think I can control my own fate and my tomorrow. I love thinking outside the box.

I listen very well but I don't respond very well towards being told what to do, when to do it, and how to do it?

I march to the sound of my own drum beat. I don't even let the voices in my head make any unsolicited recommendations for directions. I am a one man show. I stand alone, and I bow to no one.

One Day

I just want to see if I can make it one day without having to go to the Corner Store for a hit. Or end up in somebody's basement rolling smoke to get lit. I know it will be a balancing act walking down the street, because usually I'm staggering, or going and back and forth.

This one day, I'm going to try to clear my head. The last time I pulled a stunt like this. My friends made me drive and pay for their habits. All I could do by the end of the day was cry. Thinking my first circumstances were better than the latter.

The Runner

Someone started asking me a question, what if I couldn't run anymore? And before they finished I said to them, you have no idea what you're asking. I'm anointed. It is a peculiar thing that I do. To roll out of bed and hit the ground and running. It's more than instinctive.

Many times I've been reported running down street with no clothing. All I can say is, " I am sorry Mr. Officer. I am heading back home," of course he doesn't want to look at me or allow me to get into his car. He just says, " Cover that thing up and watch your ass." Anyway, I love running. It's in my heart and soul, and it relaxes my mind.

Stays In Contempt

Always there's one child
stays in contempt
to drive you wild.
That doesn't listen.
Tares your written
instructions in half
like it don't pertain
to them. Its always one that
doesn't want to follow
the rules of either parent.
It's always one child
that wants to challenge
the system.
The curfew is for every
child that lives under
this roof.
This one child thinks
that they are an exception.
Always one that has to
learn the hard way.
I will tell you goodbye

before I shed a tear to cry.
There's always one
that will be calling grandma
or someone else to ask can
they stay with them?
One day they'll realize
this is not a game,
rules and parenting is for
your safety.
At least give us some peace,
so we go to sleep at night, by making it
back inside the house at a decent hour.

I Don't Want To Go To School

I remember saying, "Ma', I don't want to go to school." And she says, "Why?" I said, "Because the sole of my shoes are falling off, my pants are too short, and my shirt needs buttons." She looks at me, the way she always does whenever I come to her with a problem. She simply says, "I can fix it."

Child go get me some glue for your soles, scissors to cut your pants into shorts, and find another shirt that's old and doesn't need buttons. What you don't need are excuses. Take what you have, and make the best of it until you can do better. Don't worry about what other people think or say, your struggles are but for a moment, If they come or if they stay, they're certain to make you stronger.

But the next time I tell you to do something, you'd better damn well do it. Or find your black ass somewhere else to live. You got one more time to let me see you hanging out on these street.

These streets can't get you nothing but locked up or dead. My last and best advice, don't let me see you outside that school, before the final bell ring."

Bitter Sweet

Bitter reality is better than sweet revenge. If it's over, let it go. Stop causing more problems or creating a bigger scene.

Just take one look back without striking a match, and saying to yourself, "It was a nice ride."

Taking that first step forward in a new directions is the most difficult, but if you keep living in the past or trying to fix something that's broke, you'll learn that sweet has an ugly twin and it's not happening.

Before I Say Something

She says to me, "Before I say anything, I am not going to nothing. I want you to think about what's on my mind, and why I am about to be mad at you."

Now, I am thinking about all the reasons she could be getting mad at me. As you well know, I am no mind reader. You should also know I am not perfect. And, I am not about to start telling on myself. So, I started thinking about where am I going to be sleeping tonight? Little things along those lines.

So, I looked up at her because I was sitting down, and I said, "I can't read your mind right now, even if I tried. I had a long day at work, and I am extremely tired. I know you want and need more attention then I've been giving you, just know that I love you. She looked at me, and said," I hate you now, more than I ever have before.

Well, I had no words to match the feelings, that she had expressed. I guess my preplanning was correct. At the end of her conversation, she asked me if I would simply leave. At the moment, I really didn't have a problem with that.

After a few hours later, two laughable movies at the Doubletree Hotel. I realized, I just got asked to leave out of my own house. I then, picked up the phone and asked her was she okay, " she says yes, "I just needed some space." Okay.

Forgiveness

I should have stayed at home, because I'm not liking what you're saying. The thuggish part of me is showings its ugly head. This is the part of me that I shouldn't have never gotten out of bed. I don't think you heard a word I said. I think you should make a 9-1-1 call, I see that you're about to fall.

Take a dollar, keep the change, your heaven or hell is calling your name. I don't play fool, your mama' and daddy should've taught you better. These streets are some mean streets, and they don't offer no second chances. Never once have I told another brother to go to hell.

If I did, that same brother might not give me the same chance. Looking back, don't let too many of the really good days pass you by, make the most with your grand-parents, and with your mom and dad.

So, the relationship growing up wasn't always the best, but you have to learn to forgive them, and ourselves for hating them so much. A lot of the anger we carry as a child, often stays with us as adult.

If we don't deal with it along the way, it will wear ugly and uglier over the years, on your feet, hands and eyes.

Nobody can make you do anything now. You have to learn to crawl, walk and run in areas of your life you never thought were possible.

Forgiveness is not a pill that you can easily swallow, but it is an awfully big step in the right direction. Looking back, one word summarized.

Looking For Me

I am liking the idea that you're looking for me. But, I don't sit around waiting for someone to come find me.

I keep it moving, looking but without expecting anything. I have already gone distances with a few people, even a greater journey with them inside my head.

All I want to do now is live for the one who gave me life, set me free and keeps me lifted everyday, Jesus.

Truly, everyday you wake up, you have to proclaim your faith, and reclaim your life. Because there's always some fool that's thinking they own you, and you have to rebuke all that foolishness in Jesus name.

My Parents Don't Understand

My parents don't understand, and I don't know how to explain it to them. Everybody I know is doing it, so it can't be all that bad. I am not caught up in peer pressure. I am just experimenting with more than what my parents have ever allowed me.

Whenever I ask them anything, they always say, " No," followed by a long lecture on, "Haven't we taught you better." Lastly, asking me for GPS coordinates and to stay where I am, because we're coming to get you.

All I want to do is try marijuana to see what it's feels like to get high. Everything is not a bad deal or such bad deal, other people get high all the time. I am not looking at it as a problem solver.

My parents are so afraid, I'd get addicted to drugs or hooked on a person, that I would literally forget that they were my parents. I am thankful for their worries and concerns for my wellbeing, because so many of my friends parents don't even care. Though, I don't like sharing everything with my parents, I know their love for me and guidance is the best that any child can have.

I Love Them

I love them, but I don't want to fight them.

They've gotten to the point whereas they don't want to listen.

I found myself talking to myself, and looking up and down the street for them, but from the window.

One day they will get it.

I just want you to be safe out there.

Please Don't

Please don't waste anymore of my time. It's okay to look my way, but don't stop to get my attention, don't even do anything to make me smile. I don't need anymore head aches, hearts aches or head games, or days and nights trying to figure out what's on the other person's mind.

Just leave me be. I'd rather be left alone, than in a relationship with so much uncertainty. I know where I'm going, doesn't matter if I end up there alone. I've carried too much extra baggage, that didn't belong to me. I carried it a great distance, just to have to sit it all down and walk away. It wasn't mines to carry.

Who wouldn't enjoy some light conversation every now and then? And being able to cuddled up beside a warm body? But, there has to be a lot more to it, than that. I need the whole kit and caboodle. It can't be when I need the love in return, it gets ups and walks away.

I Tried My Best

I tried my best on a night
like this many years ago.
I was driving and she was
with me, my vehicle broke down
in the pouring snow.
We had been arguing, so she
jumped out. And I couldn't
convince her to get back into a
vehicle that wasn't going anywhere.
So, I watched her walk away.
She had no hat, scarf, or boots.
Just had a made up mind.
I called her later that evening
when I finally made it home.
Told me it was over, and hung
up the phone.
I remember trying my best
on a night like this when
the snow was coming down,
my vehicle had broken down,
and there wasn't anything I could
do to stop her from leaving.

Dropping Son Off

While, I was driving this morning and dropping my son off to school. I said to him, after a few minutes into the ride; I remember sitting on the passenger side and my dad saying some of the same things, I'm telling you now. Work hard, stay focus, and get all your assignments done.

You'll have plenty of time to play later. If you want to drive a nice car, live in a nice house, and have money in the bank, it starts here and now. One day you'll be sitting where I am, telling your son the same things. As he got out the vehicle, remember I love you son.

It's Later Than You Think

It's later than you think, but I have time for one more. One more dig, it's your grave. If you don't start living right. I have been where you are. Your plan A is not working. You need a plan B.

Like so many other people sitting, but not paying attention in church, cell phone vibrating and you stop to see who's calling or texting you. It's the Devil trying to still your blessing. They know where you are right now.

If it wasn't that, your flesh is checking out all the meat seating around you. Being saved is one big step, but the real sinners know, it's liken unto a 12 step recovery program. Come let's go into the House of the Lord. Do yourselves a favor, stay focused.

YEARS, TEARS OF FUSSING

YEARS, TEARS, OF FUSSING UP AT THE EMPTY CORNER OF THE CEILING AND THROWING PUNCHES INTO THE AIR AROUND ME, BECAUSE I KNOW YOU'RE STILL HERE, SOMEWHERE. AND YOU CAN STILL HEAR ME. I AM HAPPY TO ANNOUNCE THAT MY DAD AND I, ARE JUST STARTING TO GET ALONG.

AS A CHILD I COULDN'T SEE EVERYTHING, AND HIM AS A PARENT COULDN'T BE EVERYTHING, IN ANY RELATIONSHIP IT IS OFTEN GOOD FOR TWO PEOPLE TO KNOW THEIR DIFFERENCES AND MEND THOSE FENCES ALONG THE WAY. SOMETIMES, LIKE ANYTHING ELSE IT TAKES A TURNS FOR THE WORST AND BECOMES TOO LATE. THE MOST IMPORTANT THING IS THAT WE NEVER STOPPED TALKING AND BEFORE HE PASSED AWAY, NOT LISTENING TO HIM WAS NOT A CHOICE.

I HAVE MANAGED TO SUMMARIZE THE IMPACT THAT MY FATHER HAS HAD ON MY LIFE, NOTHING FALL SHORT OF ME ANNOUNCING HIM POSTPARTUM THE WORLDS GREATEST DAD. HE WAS EVERYTHING HE NEEDED TO BE, AND HE PROVIDED THE BEST GUIDANCE A FATHER COULD GIVE TO A CHILD. LOVE, CARE, UNDERSTANDING AND ENDLESS STORIES ABOUT LIFE AND HOW TO BE A BETTER MAN, A HUSBAND, A FATHER AND A GOOD NEIGHBOR TO EVERY ONE AROUND.

MOST IMPORTANTLY, HE ALWAYS SAID, "KEEP YOUR CHIN UP SON, AND DON'T LOOK DOWN, YOUR LIFE HAS YET TO BEGIN." FOR ALL YOU'VE DONE, SAID AND PROVIDED FAITHFULLY WITHOUT ILL FEELINGS OR GRUDGE, THANK YOU DAD.

My Word

My word,
and it should be yours.
This year I will
try to do better.
Find it first, pick up my bible, read it,
and go to church more often.

Stop doing the things
that I know that are
driving God mad, that
are all bad because His
love for me means, I
should be loving Him back.

Too many good days, months,
and years spent doing the wrong
things. If not now, when will
I live for God?

I am sure He's been wondering
if His time was wasted bringing me
into this world, like many of
your mothers that had labored in pain
from your birth up until now.

Say' yes it's time.
Just know in your heart that God can,
what no one else can, but
you my brothers and sisters have
to have a mustard seed size faith,
and believe that all things are possible
for your life through the
blood of Jesus, who paid it with His
life on Calvary.

R A W

A Good Friend

There's nothing like a good friend

A best friend

A true friend

A real friend

Through thick or thin

Up and down,

and back again.

A Soldier on and off

the battlefield.

Someone that knows

when to give you a hand.

Someone that truly understands.

Always right there for you.

Tell you the truth and run bare with you.

Ride and die, so sweet_

They put honey out of business

But no truer friend than

one that has laid down His

Life for you.

I Don't

I don't dislike God
It's just when I see Him
I run and hide,
or go onto the opposite
side of the street.
I say and do things
I know He does not like.
I try not to look in His direction.
And I stop immediately when
I think or feel He's looking.
Yeah, its called conviction
I created this unnecessary space
between Him and I,
and I have to do better.
I don't dislike God
I dislike the things I say and do
that are not of God.
I want to change all of that,
so God and I are speaking the same
language and doing the same things.

God Is

God is your Healer
Not your pharmacist
or corner drug dealer.
No matter what your circumstances are.
So what! You slipped and fell, but you don't
have to stay down, or continue
in the way that will lead
your soul to hell.
Angels jump in your path during
your life's span.
They talk to you, walk with you,
just to encourage you when
you least expect them to.
And explain to you that everything
is going to be better than expected.
But you have to give yourself
every chance to live for God,
and not just for yourself.
God is the only painter that sees
the big picture, and He does
nothing but show you as much
as He can, but you have to
learn to take one day at a time,
and always hold onto the
Masters hand.

Looks Like We Made It

Look behind us,
while others faded
into the scenery
Where there was
no greenery.
I heard nothing because
my focus was
up front.
It's like that sometimes,
people stopping along
the way, all for different
reasons, a lifetime or season
not for me to judge.
I wanted to see what's
on top of the mountain.
I knew there would be
everyday struggles and
storms I'd have to pray
my way through.
But all the days were not
bad, some had plenty of
cool days with just
the right amount of sun.
I had fun, but not too
much fun.
The body and mind has
to stay tuned, and my eyes
never too much slumber.
It's never bothered me to
become jaded, I never
wanted to become faded.

Picking Fruit

You keep picking the wrong person in your life, because you've never learned or were taught how to pick ripe fruit from the tree.

If you're picking something up from the street or something someone has thrown away; you might not be able to see it's no good, and probably rotten in the core.

I am not saying you can't make nothing with it, but it'll be more problems than its worth.

I heard a pastor in his sermon say, if you want a fruit, you need to climb up a tree and go out on a limb.

I've watched my grandmother devourer a good piece of fruit, before she made it to the register.

The point is, how are you picking the right person in your life. No time to waste on people in a relationship that aren't ready; rotten or not ripe.

This Man's Spirit

This man's spirit, talking about my dad, seem to never want to leave me alone. I am asleep having this dream. At this time I am a teenager, just in a usual fussing contest with my mother; I'm probably telling her she's wrong about something.

Then dad walks into the room to her defense and says, " I am going to beat you," and immediately grabs a broom. I started trying to verbally calm him down, by saying," Dad it wasn't all that;" while trying to duck and dodge swings from this red handle broom. At this time I thinking, I am really not in the mood to take a whipping, so I made my way out of the house.

Damn! I know there's no way I'm going back into that house. One thing about my dad, he never know how to let stuff go. If he felt you were due a beating, in his mind he's just waiting to catch up with you or when you've forgotten. At any time, he'll bring it back to your remembrance.

Now, I am out of the house and no place to go. This is when I woke up, still mad at certain episodes between dad and I. Too late now, I'm still not taking a whipping from him dead or alive. But, he was right about one thing, I should have been more respectful towards my mother. I think he'd be proud of me now.

Hold Me

Hold me,
come wipe my tears away_
Nobody in this world
can replace you.
Nothing in this world
can replace what we had
or how I feel.
Everything about you
separates you from
everyone else.
I've tried to move on
without you but it feels like
I'm dying without you.
One day we'll run into
each other. I hope
you don't see our past
but our future_

Kauai

I miss you every now and then.
It use to be everyday
This thing we had-
I call you or you'd
call me and things afterwards
never seemed as bad.
I don't know if it
was on a cloudy, sunny
or rainy day- but I know
you're gone forever away-
Nothing like a friend
in the world that
understand you- holds
your hand and goes
through when you do.
Put your on their shoulders
or carries your weight
on their back, you don't
find too many friends like that.
I still look for you and listen
for the sound of your voice,
I know you'd want me to move
on with my life but not forget you.
I am left with no other choice
I will always miss you and forever
hold onto the memories of yesterday.

Battle Scars

All I am going to do from here on out, is show my battle scars. The knife scar was to her defense, I came at her and she wasn't in a playing mood. I should have stopped at the first, no.

Then on another occasion, things were going so well, she said something sideways, can't remember now what it was; but I told her to go to hell.

Then she took a run upstairs for the gun, shot me twice and it left me laughing and bleeding at the same time. I couldn't believe the bitch shot me.

Several years later, I still think about her sometimes, and the good times. But, the court made it virtually impossible for us to be together. I can only visit her the third Wednesday of each month.

We Said

Though we said, we'd
never go to bed mad_
We'd never go a month without
going to church on Sunday.

We'd never argue in front
of friends, the children or relatives.
And no matter how bad things got,
we'd never call the police on one
another.

All that went out the window.
I'm locked up!
Blocked up! And I am wondering
if you still love me.

I Gave My Heart Away

I gave my heart away, because I thought they loved me as much as I loved them, and my love would be able to sustain them; I was wrong_

Here I stand because I don't understand this man, how he managed to make me break all my furniture into pieces; I was wrong_

I didn't see it coming, I guess all the sweet talk was double talk. The roses were a distraction, and the warm night was my security blanket; I was wrong again.

Now I fear myself, I can't trust my judgment, my instincts or gut feeling. No breech in the wall of this affair, just one notice, "I'm leaving you."

I was wrong not to see it coming, and to have given my heart away, at the price that can not be replaced; I can not blame anyone else, but myself_ I was wrong, but never again.

I Can't Do This

I can't do this without you
I don't want to do this without you
We go back a long way.
We promised each other
that we'd always be there
for each other.

What I don't understand now, why
you are going down the street
in a different direction?
Aren't you even going to wait
for me? Look like you were going
to, just leave me.

What was the promise for?
If you're going to leave, just
have the decency, to at least
kiss me good bye.

I would want to cry in your arms,
thinking about all the goods times,
and the great moments we shared.
Who better than me, to wish you well.

Learning To Love

Learning to love someone is hard, but running away is easy. By no means stay in an abusive relationship but know when you've given that person every chance. Before you look twice outside the window and leave, and once out the door.

I thought you were cool, but you're not. You're mean, nasty and selfish. I don't know why I didn't see that at first or along the way.

Everything is about you; everything else is a pretense that you even cared about anyone else other than yourself.

Now that everything is out in the open, I guess you should be really happy because nothing is preventing you from leaving.

You've gotten what you've wanted and it's nothing behind your mask. Please do yourself a favor, find God before it's too late.

Because the next person's space that you invade may not be as nice. This one, I'm taking for the team.

I Am Back

I am back,
Legs and heart strong.
When I wake up in the
morning, it will be time
to get it on, rain, shine
or storm.
I am a runner by nature,
it's in my blood.

I turn the corners
with the wind in my face,
or slapping me on my back.
I can imagine the weather
greeting me, welcome back.

Somewhere along the way,
I'll be wiping away the
cobwebs' and breaking away
in my mind, from my normal stride.

I might start stripping because
I have nothing to hide.
My Lord said, to His Lord
"it's time."

In Too Deep

I remember the first time I saw her, it was like looking into a new born baby's eyes; something you never forget. Everything about her was captivating.

I couldn't see straight, think right; and every time we were together I could hardly catch my breath. But, I never knew this feeling I'd live to regret.

When things go terribly wrong in your life, you want to have someone else to blame, or be able to come up with some reasonable excuse why they things didn't go right.

Over the years I've never given up. And what I should have done was give up looking for answers. I know every plant has roots; so the story has to start from somewhere.

She never said why I don't love you anymore, she just stopped. The heart is a funny thing, it does what it wants to do, and sometimes you just can't will it away. Some things are hard to admit, especially when you know you're wrong.

It is even harder to accept the fact that I've wronged someone else, accept the responsibility for my mistake, and then ask for forgiveness. Whether they forgive me or not, I still have to pick a point, and try not to repeat the same offense and move on.

Where has all the time gone? When you haven't learn from your past mistakes and moved on. When you don't ask for forgiveness, a lot of times no one is going to just give it to you. If you ask for it and they don't forgive you, just forgive yourself and move on.

Three Views

The mirror, God and grandmothers', tells' you the truth about yourself. When you look a hot mess after you've just gotten dress; Gods word alone will have you on the back row drenched in tears.

 But, grandmothers always tell you to come here, take one look at you, because they can see and know what's wrong, fix you up and send you on your way.

When I look at myself sometimes, in the mirror I don't always like what I see, so I try put more makeup on to cover it up.

Purple Heart

Every Soldiers' hero, the one that took the bullet, the shrapnel, and to the many others that drew attention to the enemy and were injured.

It's a painful experience that many of us will never know. When you've put yourself in arms way, and on foreign soil, and in enemy territory.

A small badge, little compensation for a loss of leg, arm or mental stability, that can not be replaced or ever be the same.

Someone asked me to write about the Purple Heart, for the men and women who earned this honor.

There's no way I, like so many other could truly express its valor. But, I can salute and appreciate you for all you've done.

I Love You More

It took me a long time to get where I am today. It took a lot of listening and applying what grown folks had to say. Of course, I went off course but the words they instilled in me, I always had a road to come back to.

Their words were powerful as well as power, if you use them correctly, you can break any strong holds in life; and build any tower. Words, you'd be amazed, placed in the right order will make a person happy or sad. They can also help you gain your freedom, when you know you were in the wrong. I chose to say the right thing at the right time, so that my words don't lose its power and the meat doesn't lose its seasoning.

The old me, " I love you, I've always said I love you." I just didn't know how to show it. And when I said it, it didn't mean anything to me. I just said it, because I thought that's what you wanted to hear. By saying I love you, it brought you closer and closer to me, and it got me things I didn't ask for and much, much more. Why would I stop?

Then, after awhile the voices started getting in my head; grandma's especially " don't play with peoples' feelings and emotions, because one day you'll get hurt." Every word, sentences or fashion of spanking I received while growing up, was so that I would say and do the right things. Always say and do the right thing, whether they are listening or watching me.

So I had to learn the meaning of love and not just say the words. Because we all know, it causes more damage then good.

So, I want to get to know you better over the course of time, if we happen to find comfort along the way, we can both decide what words best describes the feelings in our hearts or what's on our minds.

Sometimes it's not always love. But, we can as I have learned the hard way, is to be honest with others and yourself. Love, or saying I love you does often brings more harm than good, if it's not the truth about how you feel.

Someone Lied

Someone must have lied
to you..
I am more than qualified
for the job...
Dressed head to toe
and strapped....
Looks like I
work for the mob...
If you need protection
I'm on my way...
be about the business
and ready to pay....
I run very fast....
I am very strong...
and I can take a bullet,
but I can only do that once.
See, I am willing
to work, and give
my life for someone worth
dying for....
For all that it's worth
I love my children, and
there's nothing I wouldn't
do for them, and I pray
that I can always be there
for them in this life, and
the life afterwards...
Because that's what
daddies do..
look after their little ducklings
all day.

At The Crack of Dawn

Before the reign of Kings and Queens, this world had already given birth to the three letter word called, sin. It's the fall of nations and the death of men.

Nobody wants to live and respect the painful truth; we can live, but we have to bathe in God's word that keeps us from falling from day to day.

Day one, our mothers and, or fathers failed to informed us the importance of living according to the will of God. Our ways are enmity towards God, and we find our-selves struggling to survive in a world of sin.

Learn to love the Creator of heaven and earth, and all living things. Think not to put yourself more highly than you ought to. God is above all. Sin is like your shadow that never seems to go away; pay it no attention but focus on God who is able to do all things for those that believe upon Him.

Your Child Knows You

I didn't want to have to write this one_ Spoken Word
You don't know your child, your child knows you. You
can't beat your child like you use to, but now that child is
trying your patience, and wanting to beat you.
They came into this world looking at your ugly mug,
staring you up and down from the front in their high
chair or crib, then at the back of your shoulders, neck,
and head; studying your every move.
By the time they hit their teens, they have profiled you
and know how to counter-act your every move, acute, and
answer that's slicker than Vaseline.
You want to choke them at times, because now they are
talking loud, and trying to fight you back. That's when
you have to catch your wind or two. Get back in the ring
with them and double up on your punches, throw a hook
and then an upper cut, then let them know, I brought
you into world, and I will have no problem taking you
out.
There's still some things you haven't seen, and mama
hasn't shown you. Keep messing up and you won't make
it to your next birthday. Now, go clean up your damn
room like I told you! Before I mop this floor up with you.
This is what ugly really looks like.

PEOPLE CAN BE SO MEAN

I did not know that people could be so mean, and that
there were so many other mean, rude, nasty and obnoxious
people feeling the same way towards other people, for one
reason or another, making this a mean world.

I didn't know either that there are so many mean people
living and working in such close proximity of me. And just
because they like me, and dislike the person beside me,
don't change the way I feel about them. They are still a
mean person for disliking a person based on their personal
prejudices.

It makes it hard for me to be like them. I feel something in
my heart against those that don't treat everyone else the
same, regardless of their differences. And accept others for
who they are and where they are.

God made us all different, but also in His image. We can
not be mean to God, by disliking people that do not look or
act like us. As my mother would say, " Let's not act ugly."
We need to treat all God's people with respect, and serve
notice to ourselves on prejudices, racism and discrimination.
Bottom line, stop being mean to each other, because
God does not like ugly.

NEIGHBOR'S LOVE

Flowers in the Spring don't grow everywhere. I grew up in
a neighborhood that everything didn't look so pretty, but
the people were beautiful.

Mr. and Mrs. Robertson, Mr. and Mrs. Davis on each side
of us. The Clarks, and Norris's; I can't leave out the Wash-
ington's,

Gerald's and Thomas's, along with the people

across the street; up and down the street. I could go on

forever naming my neighbors and their children. But we

were more then neighbors. This city block was family.

I often look back and wonder where did everyone go? But

I know. Many moved away, some got caught-up by the

snares in life, and a few were called home by God, along

with those few before their time, with the shame of crime.

They moved on to greener scenarios, just a handful re-
mained

behind. But all of them I still play with, talk to

and think about in my mind. I miss those days and I loved

them all. And, there's no prettier flower than a neighbor's

love.71

WHENEVER I ASK

Whenever I ask this ONE child of mines to do something,

they do it right away but with an attitude.

Whenever I ask this OTHER child of mines to do

something, it's when they feel like it, and wants to argue

with you.

Whenever I ask this THIRD child of mines to do

something, they simply don't do it, and says I forgot,

but expresses love for the next opportunity.

I just try to find a way to love them all equally, and to

get whatever I need for myself.

Until I Say, So

I didn't read my bible today and I should have. They say, that there is a devil on every level of our lives. Just when things look like they are going good, something comes from out of nowhere, and often two lanes over and knock all your bowling pins down.

This is not good, now I have to restart this game. Sometimes things go so bad, I don't want to go home and have to explain, why I am having such a bad day.

Most of this could have been avoided, if I had picked up the bible this morning and ended with prayer.

You keep giving me the business, that I don't provide food, a roof over your head, or pay you enough attention to keep you happy.

I should have prayed today, because I never saw this coming, my Lord reaching me where I am. And letting me know, your day is not over, until I say, so.

She Didn't Stay

I told her over a thousand times that I loved her, *She didn't stay.*

I hugged and kissed her like an Italian Lover. She didn't stay. I cooked, cleaned and made the bed up every morning, like her mother, *She still, didn't stay.*

I told her she was perfect in my eyes, and no matter if you cheated on me. I would forgive you and we could start our lives over again. Needless to say, *she still, didn't stay.*

I went into my closet everyday and I prayed to God, like I was going to die the next day. She didn't stay. *She left me anyway.*

R A W

When God Says, "No!"

I was not even going to tell my story. I was going to walk away and let it go, but God said, no. You don't know me and I don't know you. But I know everything you're going through. You have a child, and you call her "Baby." I found out. And I found out she's having a baby. I didn't want to have to tell you, because she didn't want anyone else to know.

I came here to tell you, then I changed my mind, after I got to talking to you. I was already out the door. Then you ask who did I come here for. I was trying to keep my mouth closed but God said, no.

Then, as I started telling my story a child came from out of the house and ran into the street, and was struck by a car. The mother of the child I was talking to ran afterwards and started screaming, but as I watched the incident happened, God had already told me, no. The child laid there for awhile. I kept telling the woman, God said, "No!"

A moment later, the child started coughing and got up without a scratch. When God says, no. That means it's not over. That means, God will see you through. I have to finish my story, her other child is having a child, and doesn't know how to tell you. I was walking by two people, that I didn't know. But the girl just kept on crying, "that I can't go home. And I feel so all alone." And, as I tried to walk away, after the man she was with ran away, God told me, "No!"

I said, you don't know me, and I don't you. But I know everything that you're going through. I was going to walk away but God told me to talk to you. It's going to be alright, day last longer than night, and joy always comes when you least expect it. After I sat and talk to her for a good little while. She told me she couldn't go home. Her mommy and daddy will be devastated. I left her there praying as I walked away.

Then God spoke to me again. He said, "Go to her family and tell them what their child is going through." I said, God this is too hard. He said, I did the same thing for you. I brought you through. When you were alone, I told you, it's not over. I told you, no. Because I love you, and I saw you through. Amen

When It's Real

When it's so real
You can relate
When it's on
and popping,
you have to
Pour some yourself some wine
And celebrate
First time
Last night
We met
Across the room
She's looking at
me funny_
My eyes lit up
Ears and teeth
Popped out like
Bugs bunny_
Think I didn't, but
I did hop right on
Over there_
We didn't ,and wasn't much
time getting to know
each other_
On the floor, in the closet
In the shower
Like rabbits _
After we finally fell
off to sleep, and woke
in the morning
I asked her, how
can we make this a habit??
She turn, and smiled;
Just buy me a carrot,
You silly rabbit.

The harvest is ready, but the laborers are few, so if you're looking for work, there's plenty to do. God so loved the world, and you know the rest, but I often ask God is this a test?

It's then Roman 8:28 comes into play, " For we know all things work together for the good. " and then my unrestful spirit starts to pray."

"I knew a man once, in the body or out of the body, I do not know:...," but when I start to feel God's presence, I want to share my experience and am not be afraid to let it show. "All we are as filthy rags..."

But, I thank God for every stitch of clothes and thread of hope I have on or in my body. All of you have been delivered, but its your choice to stay in Egypt in bondage everyday. **Hallelujah**

You Are Not Alone

You're not alone, nor the only one that gets up out of bed, and look out the window of proposedly hopes and dreams. I am sadden on those days, that I don't feel or see nothing. My bed is awfully close to the window, I get back in it. I lay on my side away from the window, and I try not to think about it.

But, a thought did comes to my head, "I must have missed something." I roll out of bed, put on my running shoes, snatch my iPod off the nightstand, and grab my jacket off the hook by the front door.

Now, I'm on the track stretching, taking deep breaths, and about to give this track a whipping. Sorry, I think my parents were a little too abusive. I remember too many of my spankings, and, I didn't think the crime ever fit the punishment.

But, whenever I get out here running, it's here I have a chance to clear my head, and really think about not re-peat that pattern. Sometimes, you don't know what's happening in your life, when you're in it.

So, I realize I have to jump up and leave out of the house, run if I have to, to get a better perspective. Looking out your window or going back to bed is not always going to do it.

A Few More Steps

Every man will deny it, but I cry when it really hurts_ Child's first day of school, the separation from my child_ I know we had the entire summer to get sick and tired of one another, but that was all by choice_

Now here we are holding hands, and taking a few more steps in life_

I am giving them instructions which I hope they will keep with them for a lifetime, all the while they're looking up at me and trying to pull their hands away, saying "Daddy this is embarrassing. I am in high school." With me , it never seems to gets old. "Pull your pants up son, and tie up your shoes."

As always, I don't think that he heard a word I said. I am going to hang around the school for a few moments, and try to help console the other parents.

Saying Goodbye

It seems like the good days are gone for good. I will never hear the sound of sweet laughter and a scream of much anticipation that could be heard around the entire block anymore.

Whenever I heard this sound, I knew it was my aunt Felicia Fowler greeting you or enjoying herself being in the company of friends or family.

I thought it was strange way back then and more so now, as I feel my teardrops roll out the corner of my eyes. She had a way about her that separated her from the rest of the world.

Always running towards you with arms opens wide, hugging and squeezing you inside. Her heart was always beating red and filled with love, and always kind words and advice; that the way she tells it, will last a lifetime.

In my heart and mind, this person will be forever missed. I was hoping not to have to say goodbye like this, but she would say, "If she could, " Baby don't you cry for me. I will be okay. God has a special place for me."

She knew her heavenly Father was waiting on her, but she was such a fighter, she wasn't going out or giving up without a fight. God himself had the final say, "My child you don't have to fight anymore, I have you from here." And the Angels of the Lord took her away. From my heart to yours, I love you.

And no one can ever be mad at you, for always demanding respect. "What you call me? I am your Aunt Felicia, and don't get it twisted. Always a Soldier for those that came in your presence. Thank you for always sticking up for me and letting me know with love, when I was in the wrong. Orange is the new black.

With A Heavy Heart

Every time I go to my Father in heaven with a heavy heart, and before I can say anything, He already knows and responds by saying, " Why are you coming to me, when you knew in your heart before now, what my answer will be? But you come late with great expectations when you had it within you to put into prayer and keep the faith.

Then I get up and out of His face, and walk away with an even heavier heart. I should have prayed sooner and often, and ministered to those I love through faith. I often say we need God but knowing God needs us to be willing and able spiritual partners towards the perfecting of His gifts alongside Him, that He has freely given to all of us.

For those that don't know or have given it any real consideration, God is in the prayer answering business. And by the looks of everything I see and hear, business is slow. Entirely the problem is with us, we don't want to include Him in our lives. I guess we'd rather go through struggles, suffer through pain, and endure certain losses without giving Him a chance, by acknowledging His mighty power and His amazing grace. Amen.

Blame

I gave my heart away
Because I thought they
Loved me as much as
I loved them, and my love
would be able to sustain them,
I was wrong-

Here I stand because I don't
Understand this man, how
he managed to make me
Break all my furniture into pieces.
I was wrong-

I didn't see it coming, I guess all the sweet talk was
double talk, the roses were a distraction and the warm
night was my security blanket. I was wrong again-

Now I fear myself. I can't trust my judgment, my in-
stincts, or gut feeling. No breach in the wall of this
affair, just one notice, "I'm leaving you."
I was wrong not to see it coming, I gave my heart away
at the price that can not be replaced. I blame myself –

STORYTIME

IT'S NOT TIME TO GO TO SLEEP. IT'S TIME TO STAY WOKE. THERE ARE SO MANY MORE THINGS I WANT TO SAY TO YOU. I DON'T WANT YOU TO FALL ASLEEP IN THE MIDDLE OF MY STORY.

THIS TIME SON, I AM GOING TO NEED FOR YOU TO LISTEN AND PAY CLOSE ATTENTION AT THE SAME TIME. ONCE UPON A TIME, AT THE TIME YOU WERE BORN, I STARTED PLANNING OUT YOUR LIFE.

I TRIED TO TEACH YOU ALL THE THINGS I THOUGHT YOU WOULD NEED TO KNOW BEFORE THAT DAY COMES WHEN I WILL NO LONGER BE AROUND TO HOLD YOUR HAND. THEY'RE THINGS IN LIFE THAT I HAVE NO CONTROL OF. HOPEFUL-LY, YOU'LL BE ABLE TO PICK UP WHERE I LEFT OFF.

AS I HAVE WATCHED YOU GROW UP TENDERLY OVER THE YEARS, YOU'VE MADE ME PROUD, AND I COULDN'T HAVE CHOSEN A BETTER SON TO BE MY CHILD.

TOMORROW IS NEVER FOR CERTAIN WHEN GOD COMES AND CLOSES THE FINAL CURTAIN IN MY LIFE, BUT WHEN HE DOES, I WILL THANK HIM FOR ALL THE TIME HE'S GIVEN ME, TO SPEND WITH MY SON. NOTHING BUT OPEN ARMS FOR HIM, AS HE, HAS ENDURED HIS TRIALS. PEACE

I Live

I AM ONE THAT LIVES
IN ADMIRATION
OF MYSELF
I STAND IN FRONT
OF MY FULL
LENGHT MIRROR
AND LOVE EVERYTHING...
I SEE FROM MY HEAD
TO MY PRETTY SIZE
81/2 FEET
SoOMETIMES I SMURK,
TRYING NOT TO
BREAK OUT WITH LAUGHTER
ACCOMPANIED WITH TEARS
IF YOU DONT THINK
THAT YOU ARE BEAUTIFUL
INSIDE AND OUTSIDE
NOBODY ELSE WILL
I DONT SIT AROUND
LATE NIGHT OR GO THROUGH
MY DAY WAITING FOR
SOMEONE TO PAY ME A
COMPLIMENT. THAT'S WHAT
I HAVE ME FOR.

Basketball

My Encounter on the BASKETBALL COURT, that's where the big boys played. I went there with my new shining Wilson that I had gotten from Christmas. Every time I went to try to play basketball, I'd wait for over an hour, and when my next was up I was looked at and skipped, told to go play with the little boys little man, out here you'll get run over or hurt.

Again, as I grew up a little older and stronger, I'd run, trolley and skip to a near-by basketball court to watch the big guys play until it was my turn next, and immediately I was looked over, and someone would yell out, "who else has next?" I walked away feeling more discouraged than ever.

I salute the young boys that stuck around until after the big boys got off the courts. I had to make it back home before dark, these guys played all day like they were showcasing for the NBA, they were right. I would have gotten hurt or in the way.

What I have learned is what I've always known, you have to bring something to the game. You can't step onto the basketball court trying to figure out what to do in moving traffic, it is a full participation sport.

The more I went to the basketball court, I did get pick every so often, but only as a second thought. We'll let you get in this game because we're playing with your ball but if your man keeps scoring on you, you're going to have to move off the court without your ball, until we're finished playing the game.

The American Dream

The American Dream is the apple pie, where you should be or feel entitled to a piece, but many are denied based on their Race, Gender, or Sexual Orientation.

When you really look at us, we're not really a Nation. We're a damnation because we still oppress the people of color, immigrants, women's right and LGBT community by denying them equal rights and civil liberties written in the American Constitution but you expect everyone to stand united under the flag, and sing the national anthem, while we're being unfairly treated, knock down, dragged, killed in the streets or beaten, tell me what am I standing up for?

But of course, America you don't see this, because you were born and raised with privileges that I and many others have never had, because we have a social under tone that everyone is not entitled to the same freedom and liberties under the law, and the Constitution of the United States of America.

Because if we did, we wouldn't be having these conversations about Social Injustices and the unrest for change, so we protest silently and aloud until our voices are heard.

Our attention is on the problem not the flag. We fight for the freedoms which the flag does not stand. I sing for freedom which I do not see. And I pray America united will stand for equal equality justice for all under the flag.

Outspoken

Outspoken, we're all a little confused right now especially during this Presidential regime about the flag and the anthem. The flag doesn't represent everyone, and the anthem still keeps many of us in bondage.

So, we fight civilly. We've always fought amongst ourselves to overthrow issues of politics, religion, and racially equality, etc. the list of hot topics goes on. The social climate can't stomach the company of everyone else's thoughts, feelings, or opinions; sounding-off you're either with me or against everything I stand or take a knee for.

The flag has stood for over two centuries with tainted blood and the anthem screams hypocrisy, and the real immorality is not to correct the wrong. We need the flag but we need to right the wrong, we need an anthem but we need words of freedom to fairly represent everyone in the song.

If anyone chooses to sit, kneel or stand it, let it their freedom that had been paid for, our is to continue to pray for our country's strength while we heel over the matters that we haven't all come to terms on.

Pray silently or aloud, ask God to hold us together through our struggles and our trials, let's be united under the flag by correcting the wrong civilly, so all of America can be proud. For the injustice that is making this country cancerous, we can cure it. Just say no, to injustice.

It should not be a matter of whether you stand or sit, it's a protest, recognize it and deal it with open conversation across our nation, not with a few closed minds in Government behind doors, thinking you all alone will be able to resolve it.

This problem is bigger than a flag and a few poor choice words but beautifully sang, when it should scream freedom and justice for everyone. Not just for a few, me or you, but across the board and extended to everyone. But it has to start here at home.

Let's stand for a flag that we believe in and sing a song of freedom that represents everyone, not just me or you, but for everyone to be proud to be an American, where we know where we're free.

The Big Picture

I am not too afraid to admit, that there were many times I missed God's big picture. I was always too busy doing something else or looking the other way. Only when I stepped back, the big picture was perfectly clear. I looked up and said, "God what do you want from me?"

Life is about learning how to love more than just yourself. Learning to care for those inside and outside your village. I know it's hard, when it is so much easier being busy doing what you want to do or simply looking the other way.

Because this happenstance has occurred many times, I had to search the depths of my soul. Lord, I found myself standing in murky water. I want to blame the world first for all my shortcomings, tell you why the child in me is still angry, and endless stories about how we went without growing up.

Nobody knows the Hymns I sing to my spirit about how I deserve so much more. I really didn't need God to tell me, that I am shallow.

Again Dear Lord, as I give thanks to you wakening me, I will try to do better. As I looked down and my tears falling, the murky water became clearer. I felt His grace once again.

He always speaks to me and touches me like a friend. I pray that He doesn't have to keep awakening me out of me sleep, but I don't mine having the conversations. The big picture was made clear, I have to do better.

Agape Love

In the beginning, we were all one people from one seed planted by the hand of God. So when we grew over time we began to appear and speak differently. But we are still all the same from one seed placed in the ground on one planet. God keeps us all protected with heaven and stars above and His angels around us.

But when He looks down all He hears and sees is us fussing and fighting. All over little things that don't even matter. And we keep building walls and making weapons of destruction that keep us divided. The shame of it all, that it's our sickness that's keeping us from receiving all of God's Love.

The air is getting thinner and God's patience's I'm warning you are getting thin. Prayer and worship are much needed to turn His frown to a grin. God does love all His people. But He wants their love in return. Their love will return them back to His hand of glory, being part of His first seed.

The rest will perish and His seed will see all eternity. Our time here on earth is only for a little while, be kind to your neighbors and treat those both near and foreign with love respect. Find ways to make peace in your home and learn to love those that are filled with hate. God's will to us all is for us to live, love, and understand life is not just about ourselves but reaching out to others that are in need so that no is suffering.

God has provided us with everything, we choose to close our eyes at night, wake each morning, and go throughout the day without acknowledging God and giving Him praise. And we wonder why there's so much hate and turmoil in the world because it starts with me.

Tribute: Coach Lafayette Moseley

We've all been there before at one time or another, throwing our hands up or throwing in the white towel. Letting everyone else around us know that we can no longer do this anymore.

I woke up and I felt too tired to pull up my pants and button up my shirt. I looked over at my shoes that have gone great distances out and back, and I got back in bed. So I can definitely identify with someone that says, I thought about calling it quits. "I don't feel the fire inside of me that has kept me going for years."

I had all but given up, until I had seen the tears of a young man off to the side, that had heard that I will no longer be Coaching Basketball, with their head hung completely down, I had to ask, what's the matter?

And they had said, you can't leave me now. Who will be here for me, once you're gone? The old ball coach found new life and made a promise to the young man that he'll stick around to coach for four more years.

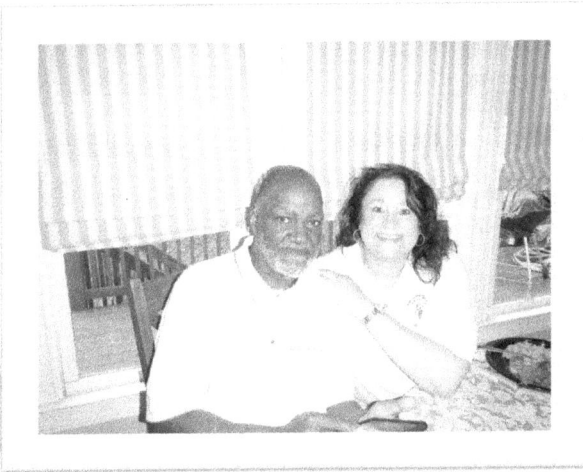

1... 2... 3

Thank you: Gloria Clarke for help making it possible by sharing *COACH MOE* WIITH US and his legacy. A man with a mission.

Poetry and Prose
Written by Ralph A. Watkins Jr

www.ingramcontent.com/pod-product-compliance
Lightning Source LLC
Chambersburg PA
CBHW070643030426
42337CB00020B/4147